How to Format a Book in Ten Minutes a Day

Denice Simms

Keep in touch with the author by subscribing.

Please visit www.denicesimms.com for details.

ISBN 978-1-989427-59-0
ISBN 978-1-989427-60-6

Table of Contents

Introduction

As an author who has never used paid formatting services, I have done the work for all of my books myself, learning as I go. Some of the formatting has changed over time, with certain rules enacted for some vendors. This book covers all formatting requirements and options for both paperback books and ebooks, including the title page, table of contents, the body of the book, and back matter.

Also included are troubleshooting tips for those who wish to upload to Smashwords, which can sometimes be problematic. I've gone through just about every autovetter error, and lived to tell about it, so I'll take you through what each error means and how to fix your formatting, so that your ebook can be accepted into their premium catalogue, for distribution to vendors such as Apple, Barnes & Noble, and Overdrive, to name a few.

Like the first book in this series, there are tips on every page, and there is no fluff. So, let's get to it. We'll start with ebooks.

Formatting: Title Page

As you saw on my title page for this book, a few things need to be included, and you'll need one or two things before you get started, or you can come back and add them later. They are:

-ISBN numbers (for both ebook and paperback)
-Subscribe link

You don't have to include these on your title page at all, but it is much more professional-looking in my opinion if you do have them.

ISBN Numbers

These are registered numbers for every piece of published matter in existence. You will need an ISBN for any and all book formats, from ebook, paperback, audiobook, even large print books. The way you acquire these varies from country to country. Since I'm from Canada, I use ISBN Canada, and I apply for a block of ISBN prefixes. It's a free service, and all you need is an email address, your book's title and the expected publication date (month/year).

Although you do not require an ISBN for Amazon, you will need one for Smashwords (and all premium vendors like Apple, Barnes & Noble, etc.), also Kobo and Google Play, so you might as well grab them, unless you're solely planning on publishing via Amazon. I suggest that you go ahead and get your ISBN while you're formatting or in the process of formatting. I keep a step ahead of the game and get mine before I even start the book and add them to the title page before starting.

I recommend placing your ISBN numbers right under your author name on your title page, and put your eISBN (ebook ISBN) first, just to be consistent. This way, when you're uploading your book, since you'll have your book open on your desktop anyway, you can just look at your title page, and you won't have to log in to grab your ISBN number from the provider (I can't tell you how many times I've forgotten my login credentials).

Smashwords does offer a free ISBN number, but then you'll always have to list Smashwords as the source, instead of yourself. When you use a provider like ISBN Canada or whatever the body is in your country, you use your own name as the source (or if you're a publisher, use the company name). It's a personal preference, but I use my own ISBN, so I can claim it using my own name.

Title and Author

For the title, I use Bookman Old Style for the font, and size 36. For the author name, I use the same font, but size 16. You can play around with different fonts and styles, but I advise against using smaller font sizes, because you'll have to use the return or enter key too many times on your title page, and then you'll run into problems when uploading to Smashwords later.

Smashwords Tip: You cannot use the enter/return key more than 3 consecutive times anywhere in your book. This will cause the autovetter error 'too many consecutive paragraph returns'. Your book will be rejected from the premium catalogue, and you'll have to go through the entire manuscript, removing paragraph returns...not fun.

How to trick Word on the Title Page

If you want to use a smaller font on your title page, but you have to use too many paragraph returns (remember: no more than 3 if you want to upload to Smashwords), set the font size to 36 or higher after the title. The paragraph size will be larger, so you'll need to use less returns.

Click on the 'Home' tab in Word, go to the font field, and use the drop-down to select a larger font size, then click enter.

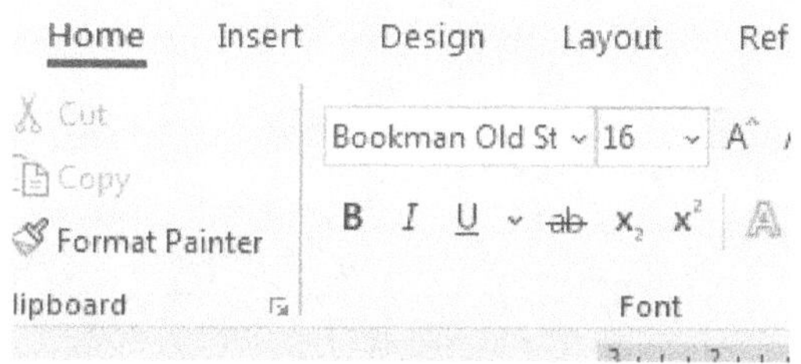

You don't have to type anything in the lines at all. Word will let you make the line size whatever you want, regardless of if you type anything. And you can go back and change the size whenever you want. You can also use this trick if you want more space (or less) between your paragraphs or in your title page, by changing the font size and hitting enter.

How to Check to See How Many Paragraph Returns You Have

This is a simple trick that I've become very familiar with and I use it all the time to make sure that I'm not using too many paragraph returns. Go to the 'Home' tab, and click on the backwards 'P' in the 'Paragraph' module:

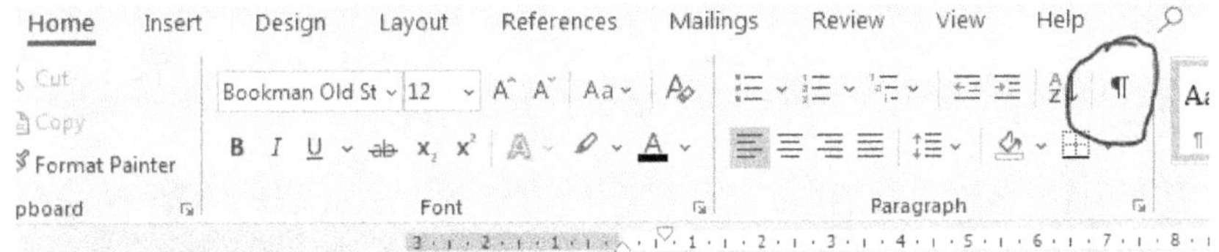

This will highlight your paragraph returns (and spaces and other formatting) in your work. See here:

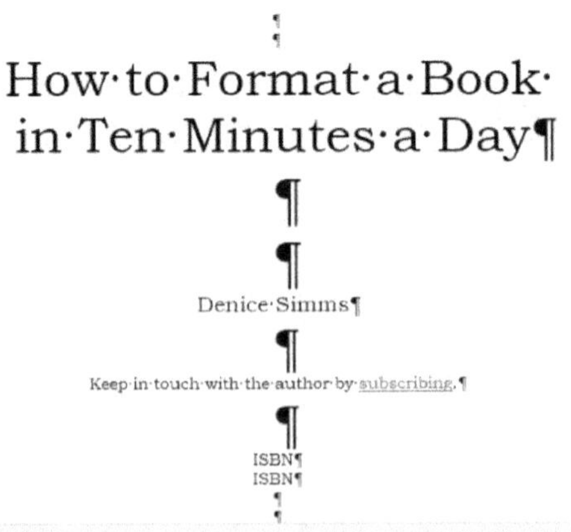

You can turn it on or off whenever you want just by clicking it again. Notice that I never have more than 2 paragraph returns in my title page? I've done this once or twice

Subscribe Link

Some authors prefer not to add a subscribe link to their title page, but I do. In my case, I create a separate group in my subscriber list, offering no sign-up cookie for this link. This way, I can gauge how many readers sign-up on the first page, or even by just clicking on the preview on any of the vendors. You'd be surprised how many sign-ups you get this way. The preview is a fantastic opportunity to get new readers, because any links on those first few pages are still live, even just on the preview.

You can offer a sign-up incentive on the title page, but I find it takes away from the book itself, especially if it's an excerpt from a freebie or from another book. It may steer them away from the book that they've already clicked on, and they're already halfway to buying it.

I'll get into more detail about newsletters and groups in another book, but for now, I'll just show you how to add a subscribe link to your title page. Adding links is very simple. You just highlight the word or sentence that you want to make into a link, in this case, it's the word 'subscribing', then you right click, select 'link', click on 'Existing File or Web Page':

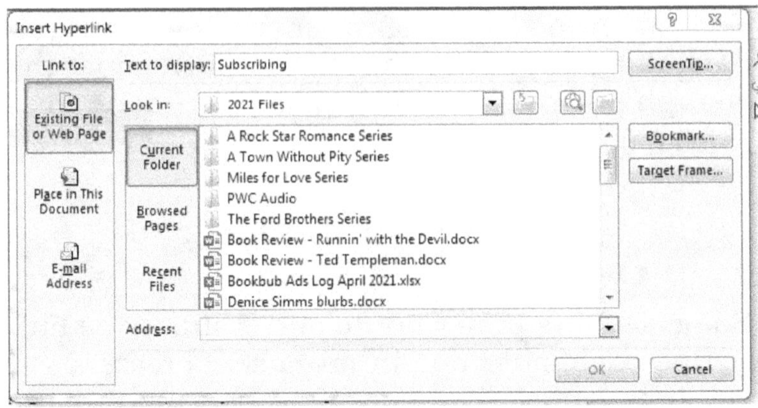

Type or copy and paste the sign-up link from your newsletter provider:

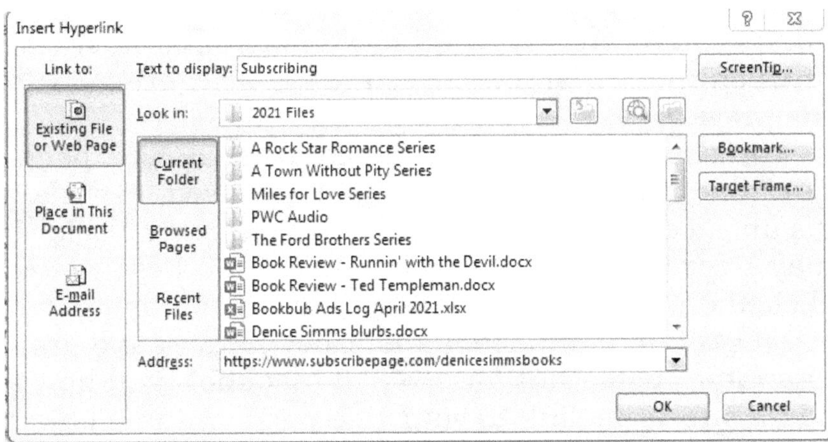

Click 'OK', and this is what you get:

Subscribing

Go ahead and click it! It's a live link and it works (if this is the ebook version). You can even subscribe to my newsletter while you're at it, and check out the steps and information along the way. But don't forget to come back to the book!

Copyright

You should always place some copyright clause on your title page. This makes it illegal (and immoral) for anyone to copy any part of your book without written permission. Even if you don't say as much in your clause, by using 'All rights reserved' that implies it. The year that the book was published is fine, and you don't need to update it every year, either, because the copyright is in effect since publication. The copyright symbol can be inserted by following these steps:

Go to 'Insert', select 'Symbol'

If it doesn't show in the default list, you can select 'more symbols', but in most cases, it will. Select the 'c' with the circle around it, that looks like this:

You can change the size by highlighting it and selecting a different font size. And this is my copyright clause:

Copyright © 2021 Denice Simms. All rights reserved.

You can add more legalese if you wish, but it isn't necessary. And in fact, I've seen my books appear on vendors that I didn't upload to, and I asked them to remove it. They do. Pirating happens no matter what you do. To check and see if your book is being pirated, do a Google search of your author name and see where your book(s) appear.

You should test it out once in a while for this reason, but also to see if you're getting better reach with your marketing efforts. See how many pages your name comes up on when you do a search. It can take years for some, and it did for me, too, but now when you Google my other pen name 'Sandy Appleyard', my name is all over the first 8 pages. Crazy. My pen name 'Sandra Alex', which was born in 2019, only shows until page 3, if that gives you a better perspective.

References

For the books that I've used a cover designer for, I have a reference that states the cover designer company name, and it's part of my contract with her to include recognition for all the works that she's done for me. If you've used an editor or any other professional service, it depends on what your contract states, if that company requires you to add recognition to your title page. Sometimes they ask that you add it in your back matter, or in your title page, but in most cases, it's the title page. But if you do have to include recognition or reference, you can place it below your copyright or above it. I don't believe there is a written rule as to the placement.

Dedication

When I first started writing I used dedications for a handful of my books, but I have ceased using it. If it is important to the story, then include it, and, of course, if it's important to you, use it. But I haven't used a dedication in years. If you want to add it, you may run into autovetter issues with Smashwords, since it's difficult to do an entire page with one sentence or two, without going over your allotted 3 paragraph returns limit.

I suggest trying it if you want to, and if you run into autovetter issues, discuss it with Smashwords. My books that have a dedication were grandfathered in to Smashwords, but I have made recent changes to them, and they haven't been rejected because of the dedication page, so I think that it's acceptable. You can also put the dedication 3 lines down, making the lines as large as possible, and then use a page break (which I'll show you how to do next), so you don't have to use so many paragraph returns.

Alternatively, you can also just put it in the paperback version of your book.

Page Breaks

The page break. It's your best friend. Use it all the time and it will be so helpful and useful, you'll want to use it always. Best part is, when you copy and paste any work, the page breaks stay intact (unless you use the thermonuclear method that we'll discuss in another book, where all formatting is removed), so you can save yourself time by using them and keeping all your breaks.

Page breaks need to be used at the end of any section, whether it be on your title page, table of contents, the body of the work, at the end of a chapter, back matter...in short, everywhere. As I've stated numerous times above, **if you use more than 3 consecutive paragraph returns, your book will be rejected from Smashwords**. Also, page breaks make your work much cleaner, and anchor text so it stays no matter what you do above or below it.

The only place you should use a return is at the end of a paragraph, hence it being called 'paragraph return'.

In case you don't know how to insert a page break, go to 'Insert', 'Page Break', making sure that your cursor is where you want the page break to be placed.

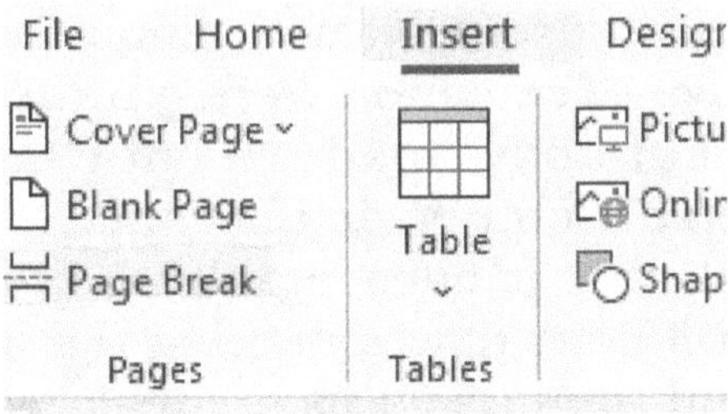

To see where a page break is placed, to move it (so you can make sure that you're not over the allowed 3 consecutive paragraph returns), you use that trusty backwards 'P' key in the paragraph section of the 'Home' tab.

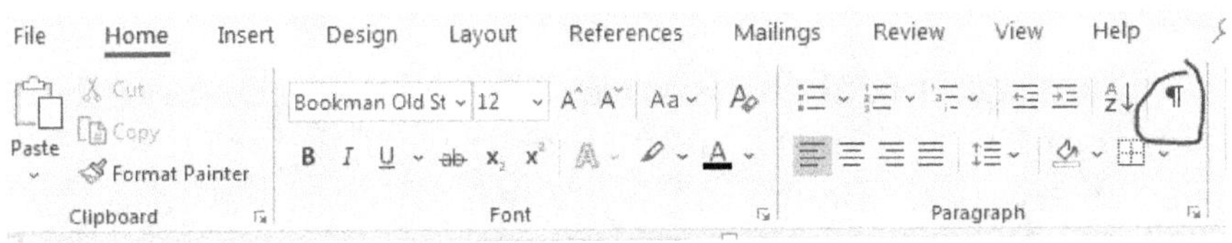

This is what you'll see:

This is how it looks at the end of a table of contents:

Table·of·Contents¶

¶
Chapter·1¶
Chapter·2¶
Chapter·3¶
Chapter·4¶
Chapter·5¶
Chapter·6¶
Chapter·7¶
Chapter·8¶
Chapter·9¶
Chapter·10¶
Chapter·11¶
Chapter·12¶
Chapter·13¶
Chapter·14¶
No·More·Time¶
Other·Books·in·the·Series¶
Keep·in·Touch¶
Also·by·Sandy¶
Did·you·Enjoy·This·Book?¶
Author's·Note .... Page Break ....¶

And at the end of a chapter:

swear·to·God·I·look·up·and·see·my·baby's·face·in·the·crowd.¶
...but·the·second·I·look·again,·it's·not·her.¶
.... Page Break ....¶

Chapter·10¶

Notice how the next page goes right into the next chapter? There are no paragraph returns? That's how you want to see it. Also, it doesn't matter if the page break is just a snippet, or if it goes across the whole line like in the first example. It's there and doing its job.

Table of Contents

This can be a huge pain or your best friend depending on how you do it. If you use Word's automatic table of contents, headings, or Kindle Create's version, you'll end up doing the nuclear method (again, we'll talk about this in a later book), which you don't want to do. Instead, I use bookmarks and links, nothing more. If done right, the table of contents is a huge resource, especially for your back matter, so readers can jump back to anywhere in the book that they want (provided that you supplied a bookmark and link for it).

You can do this two ways, but I find it easiest to create the table of contents as you go along, making a new bookmark and link at the beginning of each chapter or section. It's super easy and it's a great way to keep track of your chapters (so you don't have to go back in later and make sure that your numbering is accurate). You can also create it at the end using a split screen (which I'll show you later), but doing it as you go is best.

Your TOC or Table of Contents goes right after your title page. Here is mine for the first book in this series.

Table of Contents

You'll notice that one of the chapters isn't linked. That's because it's not complete. At the time of this writing, I haven't finished my second book (this one), so therefore I don't have any other books (not in this pen name, anyway). But I'll add that later. A TOC is also a great way, if you're a series writer, of keeping track of the order of your back matter, and it's also easier to use it for jumping into the back matter to copy and paste into subsequent books.

If you're a non-fiction writer, your chapters won't necessarily be numbered, like in a novel. What I did with this series is created chapters by natural breaking points in topics. In fiction, most of the chapters are just numbered, but some authors like to title their chapters. Either way, it keeps your book organized, looks great and professional when readers open it up and see it, and it shows that you know your stuff if it's done right. I recommend always using a TOC, even in a box set.

Box Set TOC

With my box sets, I set up my TOC using the beginning of each book as a chapter, then, most of my books have an extended epilogue, so I add that as another chapter link, and so on. Then the back matter is set up just like any other book. I wouldn't recommend making bookmarks and links for each chapter of each book in a box set. It looks messy, and since you can't create a bookmark with duplicate names or numbers, you have to have a unique numbering system for each chapter of each book. Keep it simple. Use chapter bookmarks for the beginning of each book only, and then you have your back matter.

Here is How You Create a Table of Contents

Your chapter heading should be in the 'Normal' style, no heading style. If it is in a heading style, simply highlight it, go up to the style selection box, and click 'Normal'.

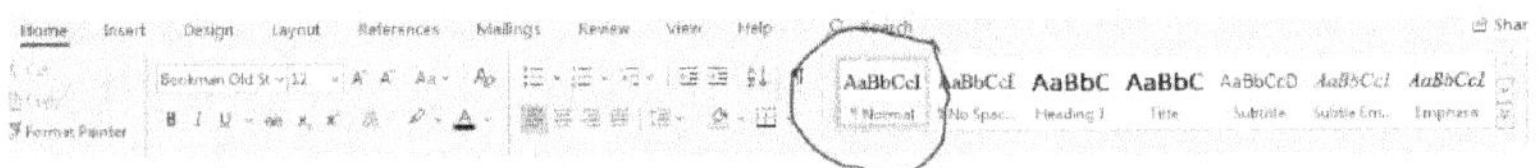

You may have to reformat the heading, because it will likely default to Calibri or Times New Roman, font size 12. After you've selected the proper font size and style (I use Bookman Old Style, size 16), highlight the chapter, make sure it's centered, and click the 'Insert' tab, and then 'Bookmark'

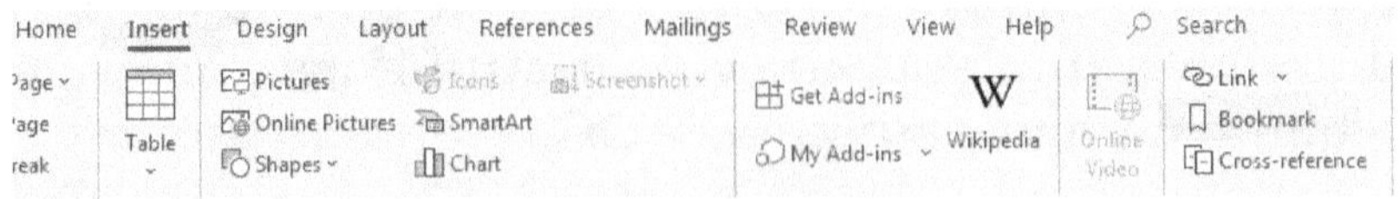

Give your bookmark a name.

<u>Note</u>: You can't use spaces or special characters here. So if your chapter is called 'chapter 2', you have to call it 'chapter2' or 'c2'.

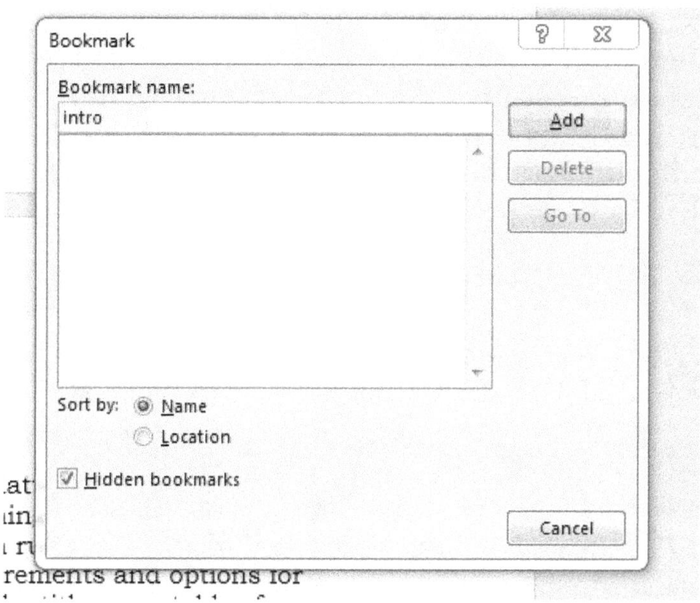

You also don't have to give the chapter the proper name or the exact title name, as the reader won't see it. For example, for my novels, I just use c1 for chapter 1, c2 for chapter 2, and so on. In this example, instead of using the word 'Introduction', I simply use 'intro'. Click 'Add'.

Then you go to your Table of Contents, which you've placed neatly on the page after your title page, and you've used a page break to delineate between the pages. If you haven't already created it, format the heading (Bookman Old Style, size 16, centered), hit enter twice, left align, and type 'Chapter 1', or whatever your chapter title is.

You then highlight your chapter title, and go to 'Insert', 'Link'

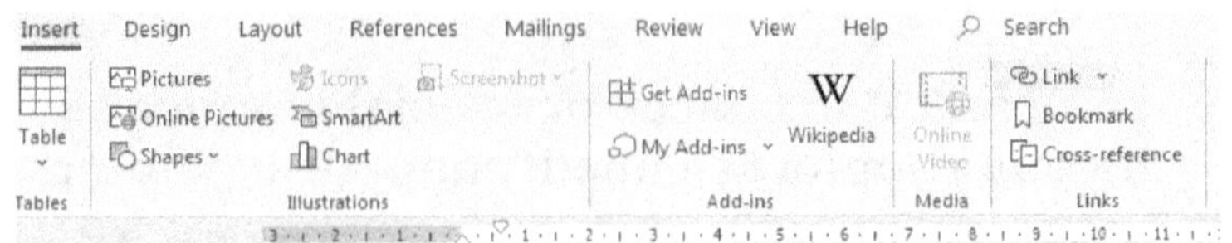

A box will appear, select 'Place in this document'. The box then shows you a rundown of the available bookmarks and headings that you can link to (but remember, <u>headings</u> are **bad**, <u>bookmarks</u> are **good**). Select the bookmark that you just created, click 'OK', and BAM! You have your link.

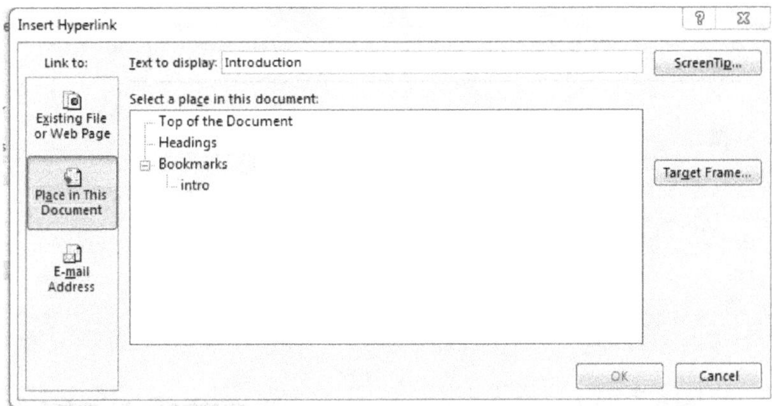

You'll notice that the chapter title 'Introduction' in the TOC is now highlighted blue. That's how you know that it's properly linked. Do this for all your chapter headings, for your back matter (like you see in my example above), and that's your TOC done.

Table of Contents

<u>Introduction</u>

Troubleshooting TOC

Once again, I'll mention Smashwords here. You must think I hate Smashwords. That couldn't be further from the truth. I love Smashwords. If you haven't heard of them, they're a distributor for ebooks, and if it weren't for them, I couldn't have my books selling at vendors like Barnes & Noble, Overdrive, and up until about six months ago, Apple.

At the time of this writing, I still don't use Apple, even though I now have an account set up with them, because their customer service is deplorable and I've never been able to see any sales figures, even for my free books, so I removed my free books from Apple and gave them back to Smashwords. Also, because I'm Canadian, I can't sell directly to Barnes & Noble, so I need Smashwords. **Smashwords also has fantastic customer service.**

The problem with Smashwords is that because they're a distributor to different vendors, what rules one vendor has must carry through to all books. So the consecutive paragraph returns? A rule from one of the vendors. There are a bunch of them, but for now we'll focus on the TOC troubles.

Sometimes Word likes to create its own bookmarks, called 'hidden' bookmarks. This is because Word has its own version of creating a TOC, which is a nightmare, so steer clear of it. It's also not compatible with any other program or vendor, so it mucks your whole book up.

If you get an autovetter error that suggests your TOC isn't working properly, and that it could be because of hidden bookmarks, this is a really simple fix. To see if your book has hidden bookmarks, just go to the 'Insert' tab and click on 'Bookmark'. Make sure that the 'hidden bookmarks' button has a check mark in it. To make sure that they're showing, I always click the button off and then on again, and sometimes the critters appear.

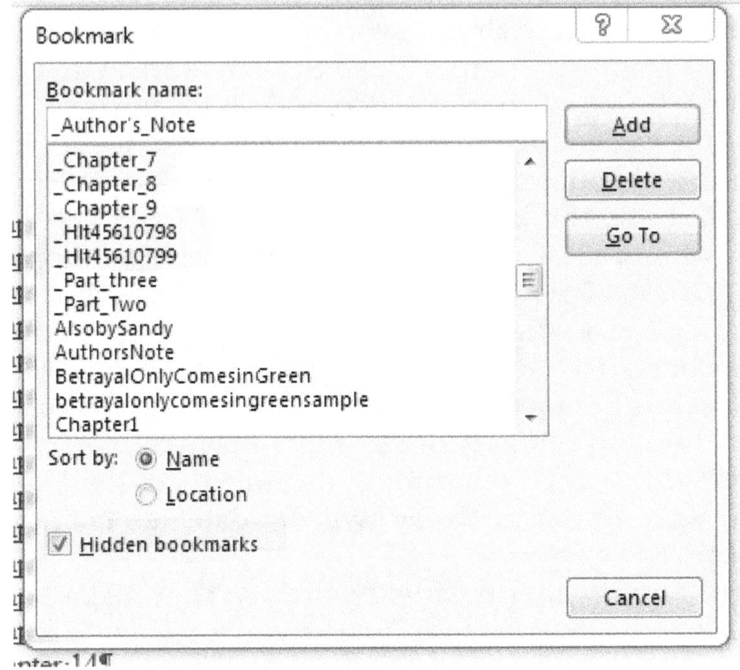

Hidden bookmarks are the little guys with an underscore prefix, and the really bad critters are the ones with an underscore, and a capital 'H'. To discard them, simply highlight each, one at a time, and click 'Delete'. Also, sometimes there are duplicates. For example, in the back matter of my series novels, I always include the first five chapters of my next novel as a preview. Any bookmarks that existed before I cut and pasted that section of my other book into the current book, will still be there, but this time with an underscore or an underscore and a capital H. They will show as 'hidden bookmarks', so they will also need to be deleted.

Tip: To save you time, when you're finished creating and formatting your TOC, go in and make sure your

TOC does not have any hidden bookmarks or duplicates, before uploading to Smashwords.

If your book still gets rejected because of TOC issues, with the reason being 'TOC not working', or, 'the last few links in your TOC don't work', you can check to make sure that they're all linking properly by testing them. If you press control + click each link, it should take you to the intended chapter or section. If it doesn't, go into the bookmarks box, delete the suspect bookmark, and redo it, using the same procedure listed above.

A Quick Way to Redo Your Entire TOC

If you still can't get your book approved for premium status because of your TOC, you can go in and delete it and start over again. This is the perfect way to show you how to create your TOC after your book is complete.

You use the same procedures as above, only this time, you're going to use the split screen feature in Word.

Delete your TOC (yes, all the chapter names, so the TOC page is blank. You **must start from scratch here**).

Type in Table of Contents, and go to the 'View' tab. Select 'Split'.

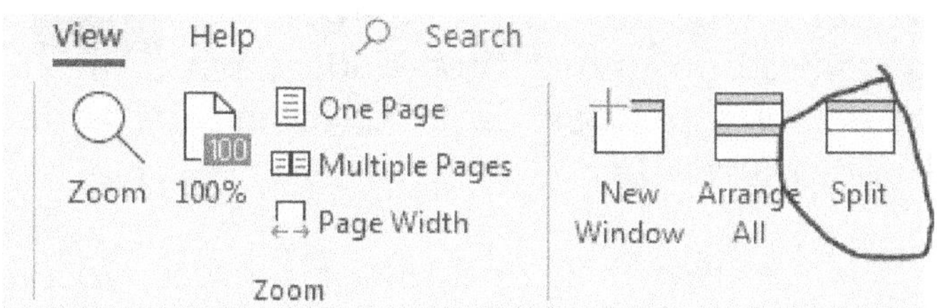

Your screen is now split in two. (**Don't panic! To remove it, just click the same icon, which now says 'Remove Split'**). You can scroll through both of them independently by clicking on the lower or upper screen. The upper screen is where you're going to work on your TOC page, and the lower screen you'll scroll through to each of your chapters or sections that you want bookmarked and linked to in your TOC.

So, it will look something like this:

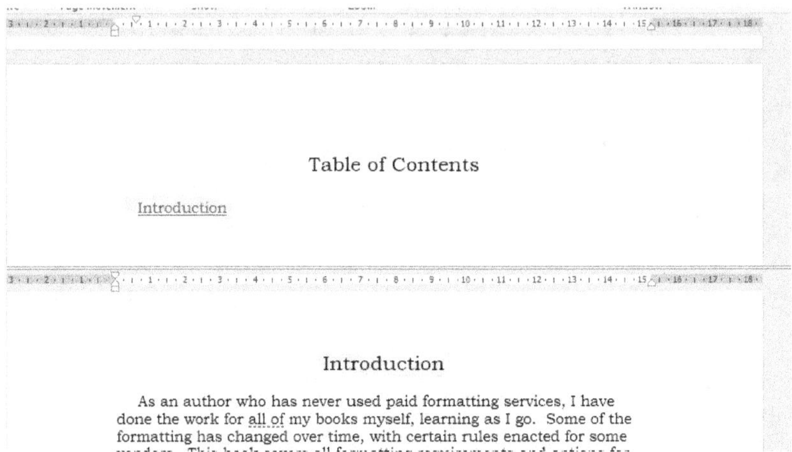

You'll go through each chapter heading, one by one, scrolling down the lower screen (which takes some getting used to if you've never used it before, but it's so worth it. This is such a time-saver), using the same steps as I illustrated above. <u>I'll recap here for your convenience</u>:

Type chapter heading in TOC-highlight chapter heading-insert-bookmark-type bookmark name-add-highlight chapter heading in TOC-insert-link-click on desired bookmark-OK.

Once your entire TOC is done or redone, you can go to the 'View' tab, and click 'Remove Split' for your screen to go back to normal.

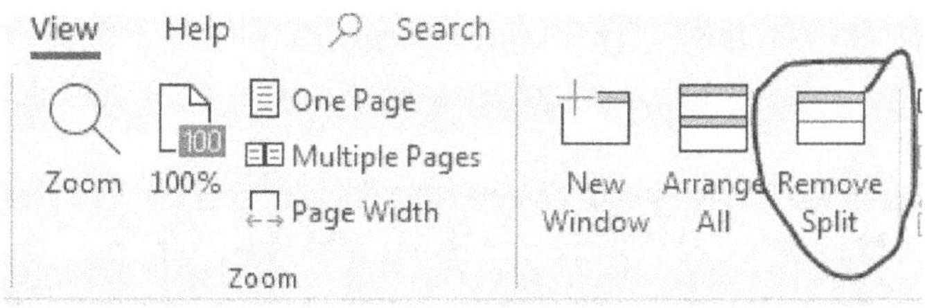

Then you'll check to make sure that there are no hidden bookmarks or duplicates once again, and try re-uploading to Smashwords. If that doesn't work, I'd follow up with Smashwords' customer support. Sometimes it's a glitch on their end, or sometimes they can take a closer look and pinpoint exactly what the problem is, rather than relying on the automated system used initially.

Formatting the Body of Your Book

We touched on this a little in '***How to Write a Book in Ten Minutes a Day***', but it's important, so we'll go through it again. These are steps that you must take before you start writing your book.

Paragraph Indents

→You see this paragraph indent? Do yourself a favor and do that from your first paragraph. If your book has no paragraph indents, and the paragraphs are separated only by a line, it will look very amateurish and unprofessional.

Some writers prefer to use the full-block style for their first paragraph (meaning no indent in the first paragraph for each chapter), and that's fine, but if you want to upload your book to Smashwords for distribution to Apple, Overdrive, Barnes & Noble, etc., you'll get an autovetter error and have to go back in and make all your paragraphs consistent. After uploading a zillion times to Smashwords, believe me, I learned this the hard way. Pick a consistent style and stick with it.

Here is how you format if you want to use the formatting style I described above, using an indent:

Go to the 'Home' tab, and the 'Paragraph' section, click the small arrow on the right-hand side.

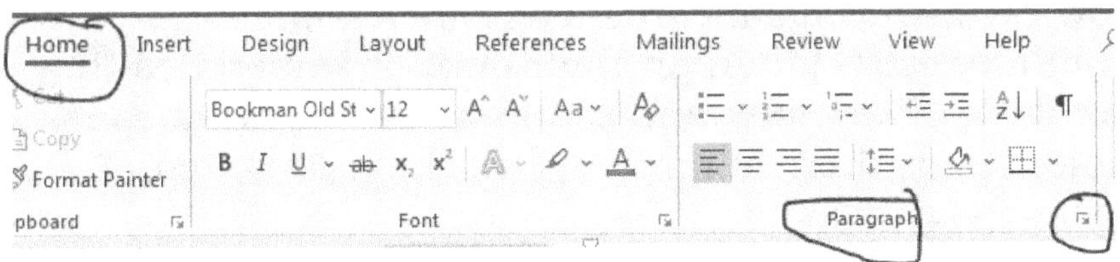

This is what you should select for your paragraph format:

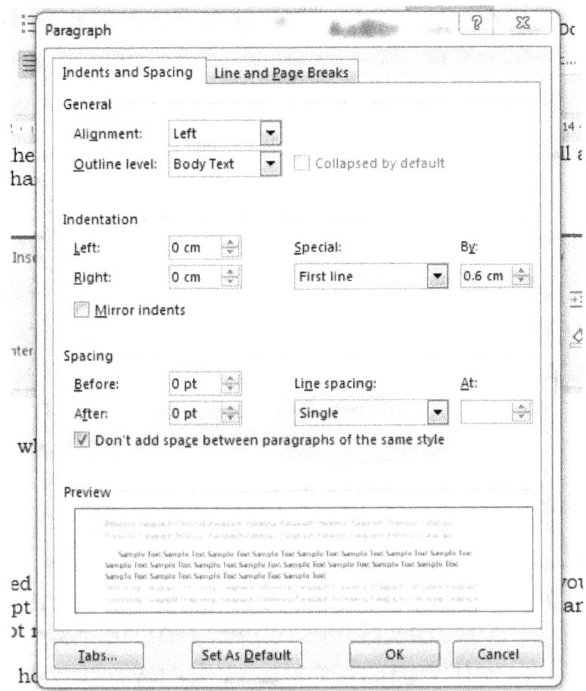

Don't forget about the little check box to tick for not adding space between paragraphs, this will save you lots of time. You can use the 0.6cm measurement or try another one if you want the indent to be bigger or smaller. I've used that size for all my books, and it seems to work.

I learned this the hard way. It takes hours to go back through your manuscript and insert your paragraph indents. It cannot be done any other way except manually, so I suggest you do it from the start.

This is how the manuscript should look:

Chapter 1

Sam cringed as he listened to the Peterson girls fighting in the back room. He only knew one voice: his inside voice, and he couldn't compete with the noise; for this reason, he didn't intervene. Instead, he opened the DVD library under the television, and selected the girliest movie he could find. As he pushed the tape into the player and watched the screen come to life, he waited until the theme song came on, and turned the volume up as high as he could. Seconds later, both girls joined Sam on the couch, as they watched *Cinderella* for the hundredth time.

Lilian and Stephanie, the Peterson twins, were five years Sam's junior. Sam was the only twelve-year-old living on the block. For this reason, and only this reason, Sam was asked to sit for Mr. and Mrs. Peterson when they went to their weekly church meetings. Their Grampa, Mr. Seamington, made periodic visits on church nights. The man never smiled at Sam or talked to him directly. It bothered the young boy, but he babysat all the same, to respect his parents' wishes.

Stephanie Peterson had a small crush on Sam. He knew this because she would sit closest to him, and when the quiet boy spoke, she would stare at him, as though in awe. It had happened ever since the day Sam's long raven braid came out. The leather twine had given way, causing a wave of jet black, satiny hair to escape down his back. Sam's tribal name was 'Springwater'. His parents decided on Sam as a shorter version, to lessen the stigma when he began school.

Once your manuscript is finished, be sure to mirror all the above in your **back matter**, but we'll get to that later.

A Little About Kindle Create

While I'm an advocate of making your book look the best that it can be, I learned a valuable lesson while using the newer application that Amazon offers for formatting books. There is no denying it; Kindle Create makes your book look absolutely fantastic and very professional with a table of contents, fancy scene breaks, clean chapter headings, various styles, etc., etc., there is one painful flaw in the application: **you cannot save your KPF file (the version that your book becomes once it is run through the Kindle Create application) into any other version**.

Kindle Create, while it makes a lovely work of your ebook (and paperback), you can only use that version with Kindle and Amazon. You cannot convert the KPF file to anything else. Hence, you have to format all your work to upload into other platforms (Kobo, Smashwords, Google Play). Believe me, I've tried it. You can't even convert the KPF to a PDF. Nothing. If you do a Google search, there are several converters out there that claim to be able to convert the KPF document, but it isn't possible at this time.

This was a valuable lesson for me, and how I

ultimately LEARNED to format my own books (both ebooks and paperback) to look just as good as the version that Kindle Create pulled off. Now I don't even have to use Kindle Create to produce beautiful, Smashwords-friendly books, because what I learned (and subsequently what I'm showing you in this book) looks just as nice.

Creating Book Files for all Versions of Your Books

After reading the little bit above regarding Kindle Create, you're probably a little bummed. I was, too. But I'm here to save the day! The easiest way to create multiple versions of your books for uploading onto various platforms is to create a file for each of them.

Every year I release a book or two (or ten – which is why I wrote 'How to Write a Book in Ten Minutes a Day'!), so I keep files for each year. Within the year I have a list of all my books. See below.

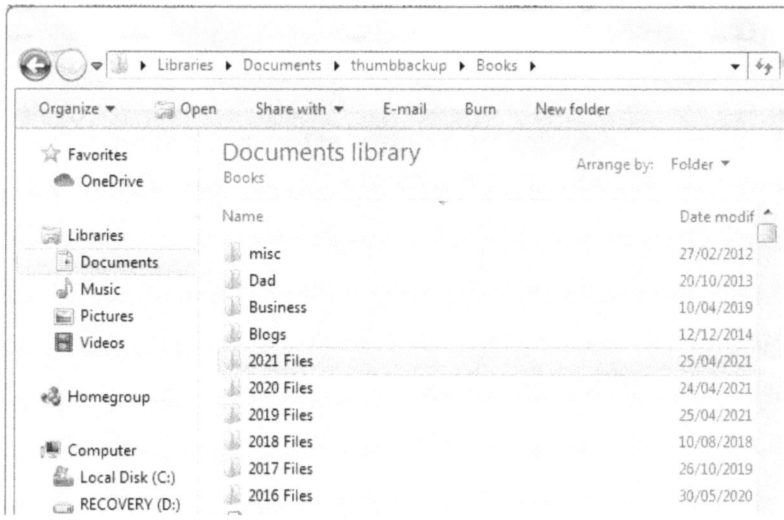

I keep a folder for each book that I release each year, or if I've made updates to a book in my backlist, I create a folder for that as well. To keeps things simple, I use acronyms for each book title (unless it's short enough).

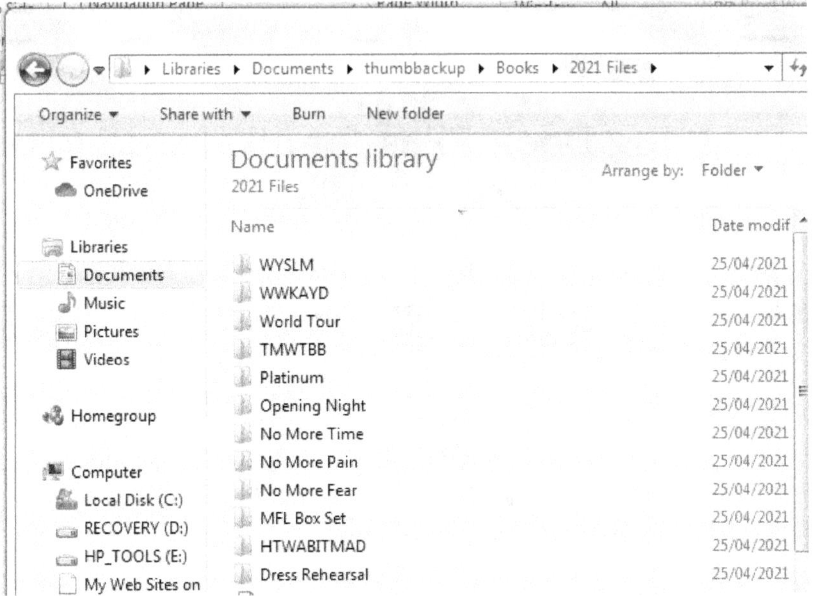

Within those files is every version I will need for uploading to various platforms, differentiated by the platform name, and the date. Where I've had to go in and make fixes (if I got an autovetter error from Smashwords, for example, or if a beta reader caught an error).

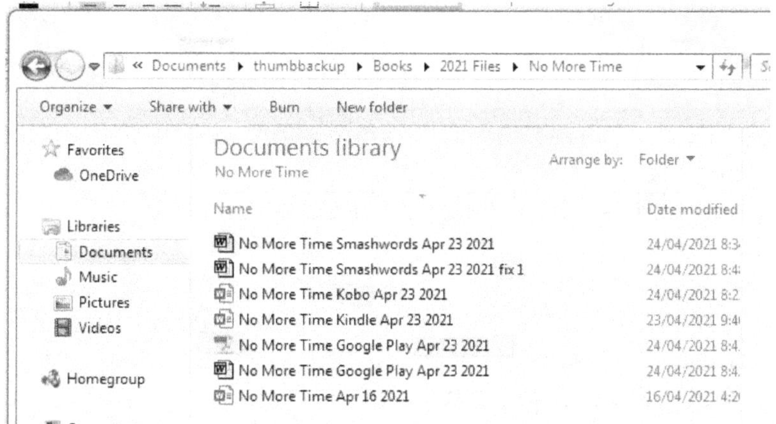

It's important to add the 'fix 1' when you make even small changes, so you can differentiate when you go to re-upload, also, sometimes Smashwords' automated system glitches, and the simple change in a file name will fix it.

Also note the file types. Smashwords has to be saved and uploaded in a .doc file, and Google Play in a PDF format.

To create different file versions, simply 'File'-'Save As', and select the file type and name it or rename it.

I also keep files for all my backlist titles to use in the 'Other Books' section of each book. This is simply a file with a list of all the books in my backlist with links to each individual vendor. By simply copying and pasting these into the individual files for each vendor, saves a ton of time when it comes time to publish.

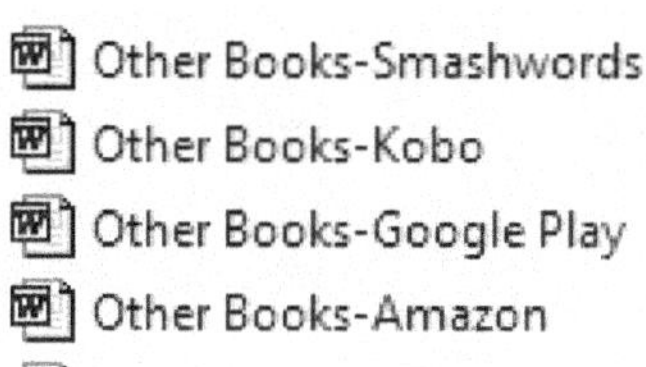

These pages are separate book pages with links for

Smashwords, Kobo, Google Play and Amazon. The Author's Note is mostly the same for each book, except that it has my Amazon Author Page link, that I remove when I'm creating a book for sites other than Amazon. I copy and paste these pages into the new versions, to avoid having to duplicate from scratch.

The paperback versions of each of my books have all links removed from the 'Other Books' and Author's Note page, no Table of Contents, and it contains page numbers. It is also saved using a downloaded template from KDP (we will get into that later).

Essentially, when creating another ebook version, I'm going in to replace the 'Other Books' page, and replace the review link and next book link, and saving as the new version name. This eliminates the need for copying and reformatting, plus it saves time in having to duplicate the Table of Contents (I'll show you how to do that later, too).

Adding Images for Back Matter

When I finish a book, the next page includes an image of the next book in the series, the blurb, and buy links (individual to each vendor). Adding images is very easy to do. Go to the 'Insert' tab, select 'Pictures'

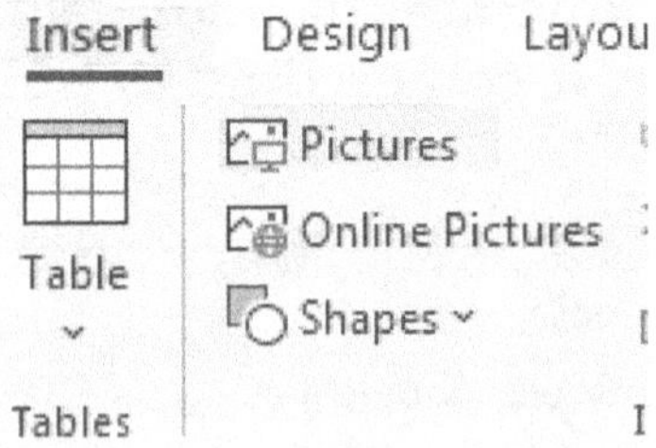

Most of my book images are in my downloads, so I open up my 'Pictures' folder, and select 'downloads', but your computer may be different.

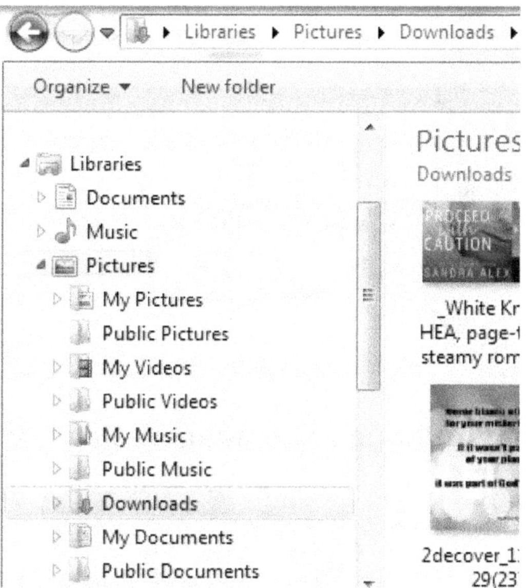

The image will appear in the spot where your cursor was last placed (so make sure it is where you would like the image to go), and it will be very large, so you have to scale it down by dragging one of the boxes at any of the edges upwards. When you have the image at the size that you want it, you can center it, or right or left justify it using the options in the paragraph module in the 'Home' tab.

If you want to make the image clickable, simply right click on the image, select 'Link', Select 'Existing File or Webpage', and enter the website you would like the reader to go to when they click on the image, then click 'OK'.

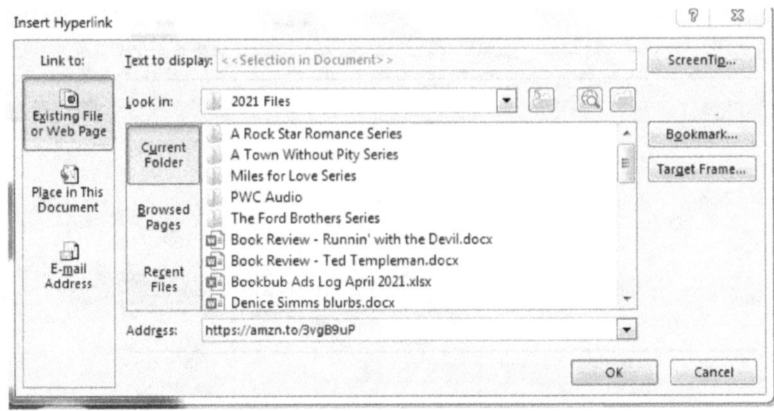

Go ahead and click the image below! It works! (ebook version only)

Here is an example from one of my other pen names, of what my 'Other Books' or 'Also by Sandy' page looks like:

Also by Sandy

Romance

A riches to rags cowboy. A hardened cowgirl. The gunshot that erases all doubt. Laura Warner knows nothing but horses. Her entire life has been lived on a ranch. It's her love, her dream, and aside from the love of her life, Quentin, it's the only thing that she ever thinks about. But when tragedy strikes at Kelsey Ranch, Laura is left to care for the horses and the land with the help of her siblings. Years later, Laura feels content with life, but when a gunshot blasts only days after she has to make a difficult decision, Laura learns that everything happens for a reason...and it doesn't always lead to more hardship...sometimes it leads to happiness. But can she convince herself that this is possible?

Check out No More Tears

Can a young widow ever find the perfect romance again? This second chance romance takes place in a small town in Arkansas, where Sherry and her daughter Denise encounter judgement and ridicule from some, and dedicated support from others for Denise's speech disability, all while a new face arrives in town.

Check out She Only Speaks to Butterflies

What would you do if you knew? Born in a small town in Arkansas, Stacey Bailey never dreams of falling in love with big, New York newscaster Larry

This is the Amazon version, so readers can click the links and go right to the book on Amazon US (this is a screenshot, so the links aren't live here). These are truncated blurbs, not the longer ones found on Amazon, so it can be shorter, more fitting for a long backlist, otherwise it can deter the attention of the reader. And this is my Sandy Appleyard pen name, which has a very long backlist (started in 2010).

Here is an example of another page I use for 'Other Books in the Series':

Men are Lisa's magnets. Kurt is her Kryptonite. Until he discovers the true woman behind the act.

After a failed engagement, Lisa resigns herself to never fall under the spell of another man again. From then on, the ball is always in her court and Lisa calls all the shots. She's independent, strong-willed, and gets a personal high out of marathoning her way through men. Until one man walks into her life...and for the first time ever, Lisa is speechless.

Kurt relocates to Huttonville to help his brother Grayson out on Kelsey Ranch. After obtaining a college degree in a similar field, Kurt realizes that horses are, in fact, his life. But the other important thing to Kurt is family, which is why he drops everything to help Grayson in his time of need. Kurt, like the other Thomas boys, is a no-nonsense, 'let's get the job done' kind of guy. When he hears about Lisa, his boss's way too forward best friend, he admittedly distances himself when she comes around the ranch. But he soon realizes that that isn't necessary, since Kurt is the only man whom she does not try to sink her teeth into.

Until one day when Kurt just can't stand to watch her scurry away, and he confronts her. What he finds out, within days, changes his life. Lisa is unlike any other woman Kurt has ever known. But she leaves out one very important detail. That secret is what nearly kills her days later. Once Kurt learns the truth about Lisa, will he stand by her side, or will he bolt like the man who once left her for the same reason, nearly a decade ago...

A heartbreaking yet heartwarming tale about lost love and finding it again. It's also about taking the good with the bad in life and in love. Pick up your copy today!

Amazon US
Amazon UK

In this case, I've include the full blurb and buy links specific to the retailer at the bottom, since there are only six books in the series. But you can just use the hook and a link. Whatever variation works for you.

Other Things to Put in Your Back Matter

In my back matter, I also include a Review Request page with links directly to the book's page, specific to the retailer, a Keep in Touch page for newsletter signups, and for my romance series, I have an Extended Epilogue page, also for signups. Also, for my romance series, I have a five chapter sample of the next book, complete with retailer-specific buy links at the end.

Finally, I have the Author's Note, which is just a thank you to the reader, some interesting details about the book (if applicable), and contact links so the reader can get to know you better or connect with you on social media or check out your website, etc. I also include another signup link here, just in case!

If you want to see examples of all these, you'll see most of them in the back of this book (Keep in Touch, next book in the series, Review Request, Author's Note), the only thing you won't find is an Extended Epilogue page, since those are for my romance series only.

Formatting for Paperback

There are subtle differences in formatting a paperback. One is that there are no live links, so anywhere you have links in your ebook version, you have to remove and either replace with directions (ie. Go to my website and click 'subscribe') or leave entirely. The other thing is your Table of Contents. In my novels, I actually omit it, because all it would be is numbered chapters and back matter. For non-fiction, it depends on the purpose of the book. For this series, I'll use them, simply because it's handy for reference.

With paperbacks, you also have to add page numbers, and if you desire, the title of the book and author at the top (although I don't use this as it looks too cluttered. It's cleaner with just page numbers in the footer). The title page is a little different as well, but we'll get into that.

The first thing you need is a template. Amazon or KDP offers this for free, and you absolutely <u>need to use it</u>. If you don't, and you simply submit your book as it is, KDP will fit it to size, which mucks up your entire book, and it looks awful. Believe me, I've done it, and I'm so glad that none of the paperbacks sold, so nobody actually saw it except me! Nowadays, if no template is used, it will likely get rejected anyway, or there will be so many autovetter erros that you can't possibly fix them all for publication.

Use the template. The most commonly used size is 6" x 9". It's what I use. Go to your KDP dashboard, go to the 'Create a New Title' section, and select the link 'See all Getting Started Tips'. On the left hand side 'Help Topics' menu, go to 'Book Formatting', and click on 'Format Your Paperback', then 'Paperback Manuscript Templates'. Click the yellow 'Download' button next to 'Black Templates', and open it in your downloads folder. Select the appropriate template size (again, I use 6" x 9"), and open it (you have to select your language first). When it opens, click on 'Enable Editing' and delete the two lines of text.

Next, you'll go to your ebook file (the one you just finished formatting), and in the 'Home' tab, go to 'Select', and click 'Select All'

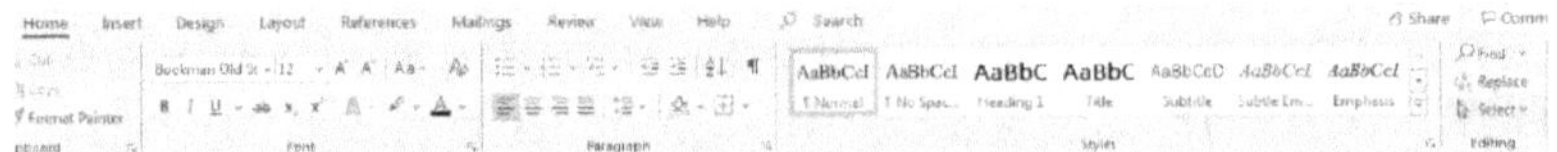

Press 'Control + C' at the same time (which will copy the entire book onto the clipboard). Go back to the template, click on the top of the sheet and press 'Control + V' at the same time (which will paste the entire book onto the page).

What I would do first is <u>save your work</u>. Make the file name 'title – paperback', so you can differentiate. Formatting a paperback is time-consuming, and you likely won't get through it unless you have an hour or so to spare (until you get the hang of it, then it takes about half that).

Adding Page Numbers

You can add page numbers to the header or footer. I use the footer, because it gives a clean line at the bottom, and makes it easier to align the text at the bottom of the pages (we'll get to that later). Don't worry about all the links that look all highlighted and puffy; we're going to fix those after we put the page numbers in.

Go to the 'Insert' tab, and select 'Page Number'.

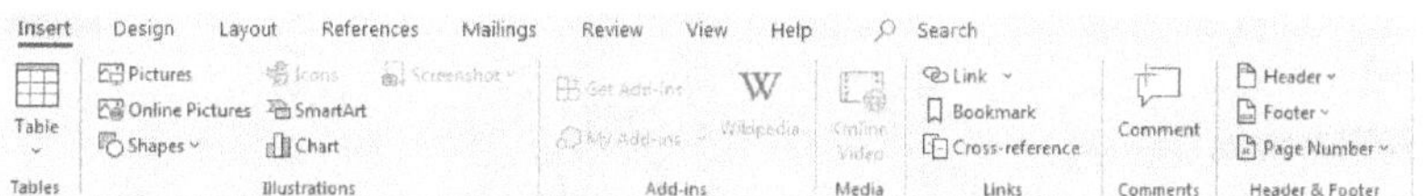

I use 'bottom of page' for the footer, and the 'plain number 2' so the page numbers are centered, also, your version of Word may be different, so the options may not be exactly as they are here.

If you leave all the options as they are, you can see that there are page numbers scattered, and some are missing on some of the pages. Why Word does this, I have no idea. The way to work around it is to click 'Close Header and Footer'

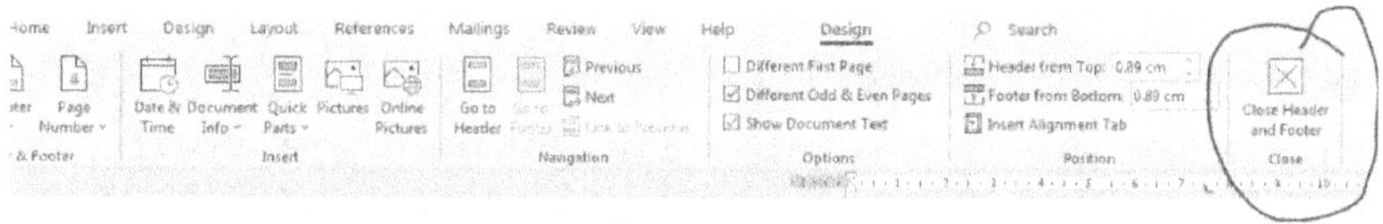

Then scroll down a page or two and do the same thing. Go to Insert, page number, bottom of page, and magically, it will have included page numbers on all pages. You'll also see that nice line at the bottom, which will be useful later. If you don't like the line, leave it in there until we finish formatting, and simply select a different page number format.

Removing Links

The title page will have your 'subscribing' link (if you included it). You have to change the formatting on it, so it isn't a link, and add verbiage, since the reader won't be clicking on it. First, let's change the formatting. Just highlight the link, and the formatting window appears, or higlight it and go to the large 'A' in the 'Font' module of the 'Home' tab, and select the black color, or 'automatic'.

Denice Simms

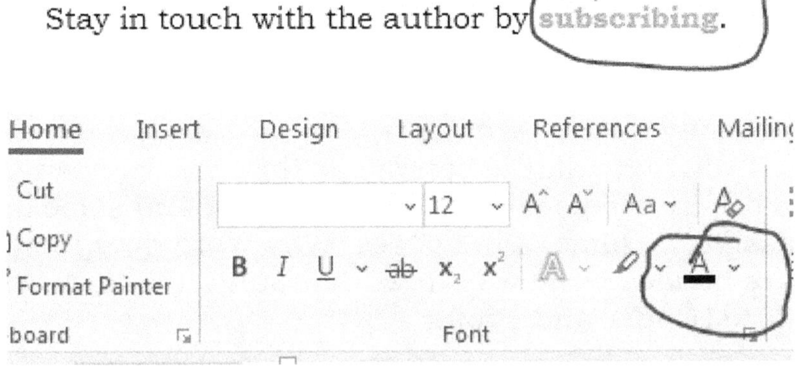

Then you can take the bold off by clicking the large 'B' in the same 'Font' module. This makes the word 'subscribing' just regular text. I would add, after the period 'To subscribe, visit (your website address) for details.'

The rest of the title page can stay the same, unless you have other live links. Just make sure that your title page text doesn't extend beyond the line, and that it's relatively centered (or the way that you want it to look).

Table of Contents-Paperback

Since all the text in your TOC from your ebook version are links, simply highlight the entire TOC, and follow the same process as above to remove the links. Keep in mind that you do not have to include a TOC, and as stated earlier, I don't use one for my novels, but for non-fiction, I suggest you do. If you're not going to use one, just delete it. Your page breaks should stay intact, so the next thing the reader will see after the title page is your first chapter (unless you choose to add a Dedication Page).

Don't worry about numbering your TOC chapters with page numbers yet, we'll get to that. Once we've formatted everything, all the page numbers will be different, so let's focus on that first.

How to Fix Gaps

You'll notice on just about every page, that there is a gap between the last paragraph and the end of the page. This is where those trusty little lines in your page number footer come into play. The reason why the gaps are there is anyone's guess, but they're easy to fix. It's important to start at the first page of your book and work your way to the last page, including the back matter, because it will all align accordingly, so if you start in the middle of the book, the last half will be aligned, but then if you go back and start at the top again, you'll have to redo the last half over.

Start at the first page (the first page of your chapter – not the title page or TOC). Place your cursor on the page and go to the 'Home' tab, select the little arrow on the 'Paragraph' section, and click on 'Line and Page Breaks'.

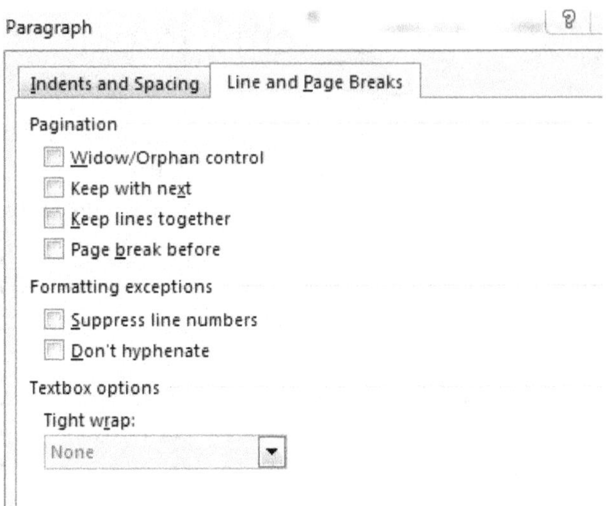

Make sure **none** of the options are selected in this box. Sometimes the Window/Orphan control is clicked, or any of the others, but unclick them all. Do the same thing on the next page, too, and adjust your columns by placing your cursor on and hitting delete or enter, depending on the placement. This gets a little tricky and you have to play with the pages until you get them right, but remember that you won't have to do this for all the pages. It's random and I have no idea why, it is what it is.

When you get to a scene break, just make sure that you have equal spacing between the scenes, and remember that when you get to the end of the chapter, that it's okay if there's a gap, as there usually is a gap there. Repeat this process through the entire book (it will take about an hour, depending on how long your book is), and it's vital, otherwise your book will have all those gaps and it will look very unprofessional.

Before:

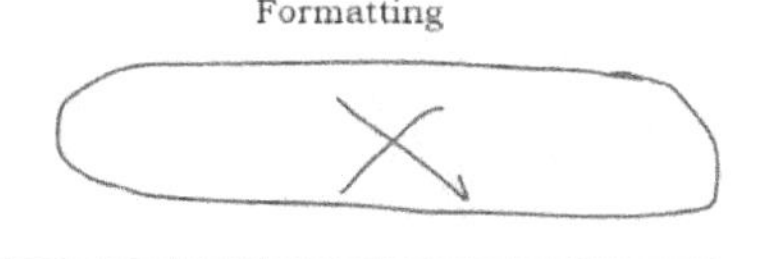

editing and other tips that I found helpful when I first started writing. Everything from writer's block to formatting to editing your manuscript.

Since 2010 I've been self-publishing my work, and during the time that I am writing this work I have over thirty works to my credit, using three pen names.

Let's get started.

Formatting

5

Most of my books, at least the more recent ones, including this one, I use the font style 'Bookman Old Style', in size 12 for the text, and in size 16 for the chapter headings. It's a desirable font, easy to read, and is clear and concise when reading. Times New Roman is too heavy and harder on the eyes, so I would steer clear of that, which most Word documents default to, and Calibri, another commonly used font, is too small and lumped together. You can try whatever font you want, and it's easy to change it, but I prefer Bookman Old Style.

If you increase the font size for your chapter headings, and stay away from using the Heading 1 style, your book will be cleaner, your table of contents will function with minimal problems (I'll talk about the table of contents more in-depth in my next book about formatting), and the flow will be much better.

6

After:

Since 2010 I've been self-publishing my work, and during the time that I am writing this work I have over thirty works to my credit, using three pen names.

Let's get started.

Formatting

Many of the simplest things I learned about writing and launching a book were garnered from making **mistakes**. Lots of mistakes. And the first thing I'll tell you before you even open up a new Word document (assuming you're using Word) to start your book, is to **set your formatting first**. Unless you want to write an

5

you want, and it's easy to change it, but I prefer Bookman Old Style.

If you increase the font size for your chapter headings, and stay away from using the Heading 1 style, your book will be cleaner, your table of contents will function with minimal problems (I'll talk about the table of contents more in-depth in my next book about formatting), and the flow will be much better.

Paragraph Indents

-->You see this paragraph indent? Do yourself a favour and do that from your first paragraph. If your book has no paragraph indents, and the paragraphs are separated only by a line, it will look very amateurish

6

You may have to go back and reformat a section with the 0.6cm indent, and remove the centering, as sometimes with a chapter heading, the formatting carries over to the text, as in the case above. But once you get used to fiddling with it, it's not a problem. Sometimes, once you reformat and remove the spacing, the next page will follow suit automatically.

It can get a little tricky, too, if the section on the next page, is larger than the space on the current page. It looks like there is a gap there in error, especially if there is a large image, so Word won't bring the text or image over if there isn't enough room. You can adjust the size of the image if it looks cleaner, but I don't suggest changing the font size. You can also break up the paragraph (if it makes sense), so it looks tidier, but make sure that the story or the material won't be compromised this way.

Adjust your chapter headings, too, if the spacing is changed, but normally it won't, especially if you've used page breaks properly. When you get to the end of your book, I would go over it again, just to make sure everything is properly aligned. Sometimes when you're scanning, things are missed.

When you get to your back matter, remove links like I described earlier, add verbiage, too, if needed, or remove the page if you can't accomplish what you need to without the live links. Then, go back to the TOC and add the page numbers to the appropriate chapters (**hint**: use the split screen view we talked about earlier).

And...voila!

Table of Contents

Keep in mind that this isn't the TOC for this book, it's for the first book in this series...lol. You can put the page numbers on the right and use periods to make it look fancier, and I've tried that, but it ends up looking too busy and you have to fiddle with it a lot more. This is easier on the reader's eyes, too, because they don't have to try to follow the dots to make sure that they find the right page number; it's right there, beside the chapter name. But it's entirely up to you how you want yours to look.

Going Thermonuclear

This is the dreaded term. I learned it from Smashwords. It's the term that they use when your book needs to be completely reformatted from scratch. It doesn't happen often, but if you either submitted your book with the wrong formatting from start to finish, or you're like me and like to resubmit a book that hasn't been touched in years, and it has all old and wrong formatting, you may see this term appear.

It's not always evident that you have to go thermonuclear, but if your book is formatted a little, and you keep getting rejected by Smashwords, or you know in your heart of hearts that your book doesn't look up to snuff, and you want to start over, this is the way to go. It's an awful term and it sounds very scary, but in reality, it's not. All it means is that you're going to take your current manuscript and remove all the formatting, so it's simply a text document, and re-format it from the title page to the back matter.

If you are starting from scratch, with no formatting at all, other than chapter breaks, you can do this, too, and it will make for an easier go at it, with a clean slate. Also, if you have an old book that you've changed or updated with a different POV or new characters, or a change in the plot, but it's an old book that hasn't been formatted in years, this is probably the way to go, too.

Since you now know how to format a book, the worst part is over, and this will just be practice. So here goes.

Notepad

Anyone who has Microsoft Office or Word will have Notepad. If you go to your 'Start' menu, you'll see it there. Your start menu should be the icon on the lower left hand corner of your computer. If you click on it and scroll up, Notepad should be one of the first options list. Click on it and open it. All it is is a blank screen, right? Now you're going to open your book with the ill-fated formatting. In the 'Home' tab, go to the 'Editing' module and click 'Select', then 'Select All'. Click 'Control + C', which copies your entire document to your clipboard. Then go to Notepad, click on it and press 'Control + V', to paste the contents of the clipboard to Notepad.

Your book is all there. Just the text though. It's naked and without any formattnig. Scroll all the way to the top, and you should see your title page and TOC there.

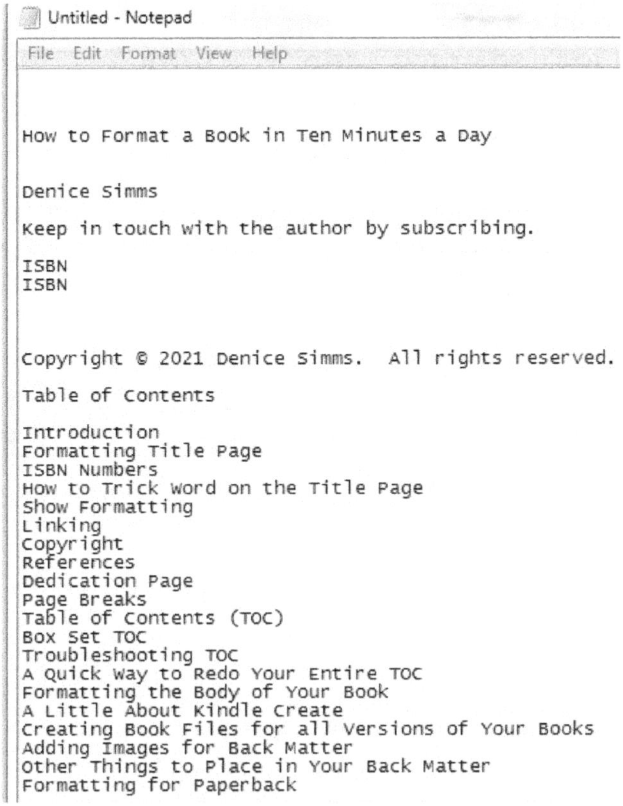

Untitled - Notepad

File Edit Format View Help

```
How to Format a Book in Ten Minutes a Day

Denice Simms

Keep in touch with the author by subscribing.

ISBN
ISBN

Copyright © 2021 Denice Simms.  All rights reserved.

Table of Contents

Introduction
Formatting Title Page
ISBN Numbers
How to Trick Word on the Title Page
Show Formatting
Linking
Copyright
References
Dedication Page
Page Breaks
Table of Contents (TOC)
Box Set TOC
Troubleshooting TOC
A Quick Way to Redo Your Entire TOC
Formatting the Body of Your Book
A Little About Kindle Create
Creating Book Files for all Versions of Your Books
Adding Images for Back Matter
Other Things to Place in Your Back Matter
Formatting for Paperback
```

Next, you want to open a new Word document. Then, in your naked Notepad document, click 'Edit', 'Select All', and then 'Control + C' to copy it to the clipboard. In your new Word document, click 'Control + V' to paste it all into the document. There is your book, with all formatting removed, so you can start from scratch and have no remaining background Word problems, or any issues from old versions or corrupt formatting. What you just did was erase all formatting, whether it was correct or corrupt, so you can start fresh.

Where Do I Start?

You probably want to hit me right now, don't you. Please don't hate me. And believe me, after having done this a few times, it's really not that bad. Best part, your book will look so much better when you're done, and you'll be just about guaranteed to be accepted into the premium catalogue now, provided that you follow all the guidelines in this book.

So, where to start. The easiest thing to do at this point is to set your paragraph and font style. Go to the 'Home' tab, to the 'Editing' module, click 'Select', then 'Select All', and the small arrow in the 'Paragraph' module to set your paragraph style as shown below.

Then, click, 'Select', 'Select All' again, and set your font style as shown below.

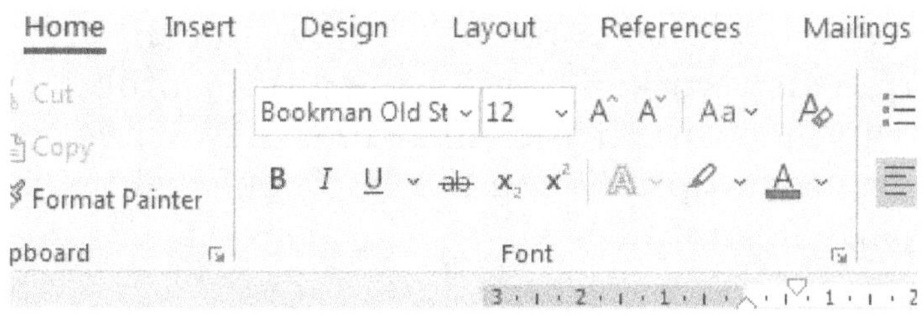

We'll tweak everything as we go along, so not to worry. Next, you'll format your title page, using the larger 36 font size, and no more than 3 lines (or 3 paragraph returns). Remember that you can set your line size to whatever you want, if you need to make your spaces larger. Insert your subscribe link, format your copyright icon (set the size properly), and don't forget to put your page break at the bottom of the title page.

The TOC you can format the heading, and place the chapter titles where you want them, but I suggest that in this case, you use the quick TOC method, with the split screen, and do that last, so you can focus on one thing at a time. Make sure you place your page break at the end of the TOC, too. Next, Chapter headings. You'll have to change the font size and center those. Make sure your scene breaks are adjusted, too, and be careful to watch out for them, because they'll be just tiny stars between text (unless you used something different).

When you get to the end of your chapters, make sure that you use the page breaks. Keep going along through your entire book, tweaking each chapter bit by bit. Your 'pg up' (page up) and 'pg dn' (page down) buttons are very helpful here, so you don't have to scroll through everything at a snail's pace. Check your back matter, too, make sure page breaks are inserted, page titles are centered, and links are replaced. You'll also have to re-insert images and resize them, too.

After your book is completely reformatted, go back to your TOC and follow the steps I showed you before, using the split screen view. See? Now, how bad was that? Your book looks beautiful now, doesn't it?! This technique also works if you've used unfavorable formatting, too, like if you don't like the way your book is set up, or you published the book before knowing how to properly format.

Autovetter Errors - Smashwords

If you've been paying attention, you're going to have to get used to the phrase 'Autovetter Errors', because you're going to see it a lot once you start uploading, especially, like I've said many times, with Smashwords. Here are some key things to avoid so you don't get any errors:

1)**No numbered lists**. See this list? It's not a numbered list, it's been manually entered. Word likes to assume that when you type 1. In the left hand margin, that it will be a numbered list, so you have to turn that off.

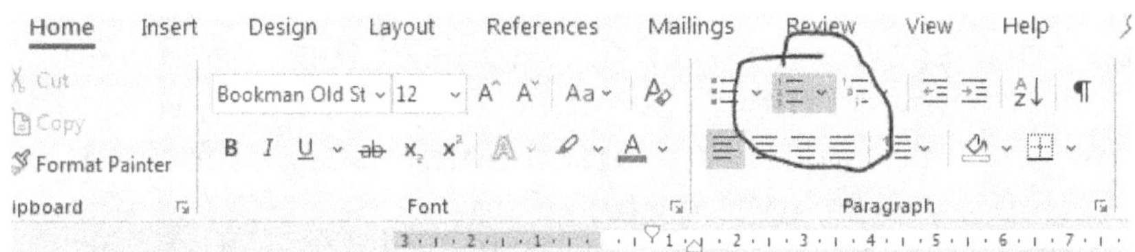

Highlight the number on your 'list' and click the numbered list icon in the 'Paragraph' module. Select 'none'. Then just use a 1), no period, no space, or it will default to a numbered list, and good luck getting it off! I did it here and what a pain! **The same rule applies for bullet points**. Not allowed. Use a hypen or nothing at all.

2)**Too many consecutive paragraph returns**. We've

discussed this in length, but to reiterate, no more than 3 returns. To find them, use the backwards 'P', remove the extras, and if you need more space, make your line larger by increasing your font size.

3)**Inconsistent Paragraph Styling**. We touched on this in the beginning. The idea here is that you can have only one paragraph style throughout your entire book. Meaning, you either have an indent in all your paragrapsh or in none of them, there is no in-between allowed. Also, if you're going to have lines between all your paragraphs, that's fine, but make sure you don't switch to no lines and in indent halfway through.

4)**No retailer links**. I've seen this about a hundred times. You cannot link to any other retailer than Smashwords in your book. You can avoid having this problem by using a different version of your book for each retailer, including Smashwords.

5)**TOC corrupt**. This is a very common one, too. It's easy to fix. We've discussed this at length, too. First try checking for hidden bookmarks, then for duplicates, and then try testing each one to make sure that it links properly. If that doesn't work, use the quick method and redo your TOC...it's not that bad!

You have the basics here, but I'll dive into much more detail in my next book, ***'How to Self-Publish in Ten Minutes a Day'***. This book will include instructions on how to upload your books on all retailer platforms, what to do when things go wrong and how to fix them, and much more, including keywords, categories, and step-by-step instructions on how to upload.

I hope you learned a lot from this, and have an appreciation for the work that's involved in self-publishing. It's not for everyone, and this book doesn't even scratch the surface for the amount of tasks involved, but it's a start! Have fun formatting!

Denice Simms

My book is written and formatted, now what? I have no idea where to start so it gets published and I can show my work to the world!

Is this you?

If you've poured your heart out on paper, whether it be writing a fiction novel or a non-fiction book, and you're not sure where or how to self-publish, this book is for you.

In this concise, easy-to-follow book, I take you step-by-step through each retailer site (Amazon Kindle, KDP (paperback), Kobo, Smashwords, Google Play) and show you exactly how to upload your book to maximize your sales through optimizing metadata.

Topics Included:

The ITIN
How to Optimize Metadata
The Blurb
Title
Pen Names
Keywords
Categories
Amazon Author Central
Uploading to KDP
Pre-Ordering or Ready to Release?
Price-Matching: Beware!
Uploading Your Paperback to KDP
Uploading to Kobo
Uploading to Smashwords
Uploading to Google Play
Adding Review Links
Buy Your Book!
Autovetter Errors
...and more!

Since 2010, my twenty-plus works have been self-published, learning many things the hard way, which I will demystify for you in this book.

'***How to Self-Publish a Book in Ten Minutes a Day***' shows you simplified ways to upload your ebook and paperback onto all the retailer platforms, adding useful hints where needed so your book ends up where it should be, looking as it should.

There are no gimmicks in here, no fluff, just quick, easy, concise actions a writer can take to get that book published like the professionals!

Other Books in the Series

Denice Simms

Focused. Driven. Creative. Got a message but need guidance on how to harness thoughts and channel words to paper.

Sound like you?

If you have a story idea in mind, whether it be fact or fiction, but you have little time to sit down and get those words recorded, this book is for you.

With a long list of series and standalone novels, plus a couple of memoirs, but a full-time job, a family and a house to contend with, I've found ways to beat the clock, to grasp all that creative energy and put it on paper, and this book shares all my secrets in that department.

Topics included:

Basic Formatting (things you need to know before you start writing to save you time and frustration)
Tools
Creating a Reference Document
Hooking
Review and Writer's Block
Tense and POV
Writing Techniques
What Do You Do When Your Book is Done?
The Lull
Back Matter
Editing (basic)
10 Common Mistakes Made in Your First Draft
What Do You Do When You're Stuck Writing a Scene?
Five Key Elements to Writing a Gripping Story
The First Paragraph
Luck is What You Have Left After You Give 100%

This book will not show you how to get rich quick by writing, nor will it show you how to write a book in ten minutes. FYI, there is NO get rich quick in writing, unless you're a celebrity, know important people in the world, or you're one in a zillion writers who have overnight success. With a writing background that began in 2010 and still working a full-time job, I can attest that the literary world is not a goldmine, otherwise everyone would be doing it and sticking to it.

'***How to Write a Book in Ten Minutes a Day'*** is for those who love to write, want to see their book published, but need guidance on how to get that pen to paper on a daily basis, even if they only have ten minutes a day to do it in.

There are no gimmicks in here, no fluff, just quick, easy, concise actions a writer can take to get that book done!

Keep in Touch!

Join my free newsletter and know about new releases.

It's absolutely free, there are no strings attached, your information is completely confidential, and you can unsubscribe any time.

All you need is an email address.

To join my newsletter, just visit www.denicesimms.com.

Did you enjoy this book? You can make a big difference.

Do you know what the difference between an author that sells a few copies of their book a month and a New York Times bestselling author is?

The answer is clear and simple: **REVIEWS**

Don't believe me?

Take a look at any NYT bestselling author and a regular author (like me) and see the difference in the number of reviews.

The fact is clear: **reviews lead to sales. Sales lead to bestseller charts.**

One other simple fact is that many advertisers *won't look at a book* unless it has a minimum of 50 book reviews.

That's where you come in. **I need your help**.

Honest reviews of my books help bring them to the attention of other readers.

If you've enjoyed this book, I would be very grateful if you could spend just five minutes leaving a review (it can be as short as a like).

Thanks very much,

Denice

Author's Note

Thanks so much for reading '***How to Format a Book in Ten Minutes a Day***'! I truly hope that you were able to garner some knowledge from it! This book comes from years of making mistakes, wasting money, and feeling like a failure. But as you can see, it takes perseverance and time to get anywhere in the literary world. And you'll get there!

If you've written your book, formatted it and are ready to move on to uploading and self-publishing, check out my next book. I've done this a time or two!

Happy Reading and Writing! And thanks for your support!

Denice

www.ingramcontent.com/pod-product-compliance
Lightning Source LLC
LaVergne TN
LVHW010944110826
845149LV00013B/2750
* 9 7 8 1 9 8 9 4 2 7 6 0 6 *